Small and Simple

THINGS

Small and Simple

THINGS

MARJORIE PAY HINCKLEY

**DESERET
BOOK**

Salt Lake City, Utah

Library of Congress Cataloging-in-Publication Data

Hinckley, Marjorie Pay.
  Small and simple things / Marjorie Pay Hinckley.
      p.   cm.
ISBN 1-59038-185-8
  1. Christian life—Mormon authors. 2. Mormon women—Religious life.
I. Title.
  BX8656.H575 2003
  248.4'893—dc22

                                                              2003014822

Printed in the United States of America   72076
Publishers Printing, Salt Lake City, UT

10   9   8

Alma said,

"By small and simple things
are great things brought to pass."

Alma 37:6

I couldn't possibly have understood this when I was young like I do now. When we look back on decades of life we see that the seemingly insignificant things we do over and over actually weave the pattern of our lives. And if those small and simple things are good, we will end up having lived a fulfilling life—and that is a great thing!

Who knows but that something wonderful may happen today. Have faith that it will. After all, every morning is a chance at a new day!

Mine is the sunlight! Mine is the morning
Born of the one light Eden saw play!
Praise with elation, praise ev'ry morning,
God's re-creation of the new day!

Eleanor Farjeon, "Morning Has Broken"

When our children were all at home and making bread was part of the routine, a friend found an antique bread mixer for me. It was a simple bucket with a hook attached to a handle. A clamp secured it to the table and it was operated by the children, who took turns "spelling each other off" as we did away with the old method of kneading. It is one of the objects that remains a family treasure because of the part it played in our communal venture of bread making. Even still, the smell of bread baking somehow slows down the world and feeds my soul in a small and simple way.

Wheat Bread

Dissolve 2 packages dry yeast in $1/2$ cup water with $1/2$ tablespoon honey or sugar. Mix the following ingredients (with the dissolved yeast) in bread mixer:

ingredients

$3 1/2$ cups warm water
$1 1/2$ cups dry powdered milk
1 cup oil
4 eggs, beaten
$3/4$ cup honey
2 tablespoons salt
1 or 2 cups white flour
About 10 cups whole wheat flour

After kneading in a bread mixer, let rise until doubled. Divide into 6 small loaves. Knead and shape. Let rise in greased pans. Preheat oven to 400° F. Reduce to 300° F. and bake 1 hour.

*J*ust be one more voice to say that
God lives and that this is His work.
That will bring satisfaction.

*For verily, verily, I say unto you
that ye are called to lift up your
voices as with the sound of a
trump, to declare my gospel.*

D&C 33:2

7

The trick is to enjoy life. Don't wish away
your days, waiting for better ones ahead.

Not that I speak in respect of want: for I have learned, in whatsoever state I am, therewith to be content.

Philippians 4:11

$\mathcal{S}$ome years ago I had a friend who decided at the age of fifty that she was going to learn to play the piano. She courageously started out with *Thompson's Book I.* Each morning she went to the church at seven o'clock, where she would practice on the piano and, later, on the organ. After about a year they asked her to play a special number for one of the Relief Society lessons. She said she didn't feel ready, to give her another three months. The three months passed, and she consented to play a special number that she had memorized. This was her first public appearance on the piano. She started out beautifully. It went well for about three measures; then she lost it. Everything went blank. Her music teacher, who was present, said, "Don't be ruffled. Just start over." She started over and made it all the way through without a single mistake.

We have never loved my friend more than we did that morning. Perhaps it was because she faltered a little in the beginning and we were all pulling for her, saying to ourselves, "Come on, we know you can do it." If her performance had been flawless from the start, we might all have been defensive and said, "Oh well, she can learn to play the piano because her husband is the kind who will get his own breakfast while she practices and her children don't make demands on her" and so on and so on and so on. As it was, she faltered a little, and we loved her the more. That experience has given me great comfort. I figure that if I fall a little short of what is expected of me, perhaps my sisters in the gospel will be compassionate and love me for trying.

Thee lift me and I'll lift thee
and we'll both ascend together.

John Greenleaf Whittier

It is good to kneel as a family and to hear daily expressions of gratitude to our Heavenly Father for the blessings we enjoy. The Lord intended His children to enjoy the good things of life. With all that we have, we must also have grateful hearts. We must teach our children not to take all that they have for granted. *Thank you* is a wonderful phrase. Use it. It will add stature to your soul. Never let a day go by without saying thank you to someone for something—and especially to your Heavenly Father.

And he who receiveth all things with thankfulness
shall be made glorious; and the things of this earth shall
be added unto him, even an hundred fold, yea, more.

D&C 78:19

*I*f there is one fundamental doctrine in Mormonism it is that man is an individual created in the likeness of God, with divinely bestowed moral agency, and that the development of the human individual soul is so important a thing that God himself has called it His greatest work and glory.

Wherefore . . . Satan rebelled against me, and sought to destroy the agency of man, which I, the Lord God, had given him.

Moses 4:3

This is my work and my glory—to bring to pass the immortality and eternal life of man.

Moses 1:39

Sometimes the pattern of life seems a little monotonous—and discouraging. It is like climbing a mountain and, after reaching the top, getting knocked back down to the bottom to climb it again; but I guess the fun is in climbing and not in arriving. I hope so!

Life, believe, is not a dream
So dark, as sages say;
Oft a little morning rain
Foretells a pleasant day.

Charlotte Bronte, "Life," 1846, st.1

You should see my copy of the Book of Mormon! The pages from First Nephi to the brass plates are dog-eared. The rest are reasonably worn. I think I have started the Book of Mormon a few more times than I have finished it!

> *Stick to a task,*
> *'Til it sticks to you.*
> *Beginners are many,*
> *Finishers are few.*
>
> Anonymous

The gospel of Jesus Christ is the greatest force for peace and unity on the face of the earth and, when every knee shall bend and every tongue confess that Jesus is the Christ, there will be no divisions among us.

And this shall be the sound of his trump, saying to all people, both in heaven and in earth, and that are under the earth—for every ear shall hear it, and every knee shall bow, and every tongue shall confess, while they hear the sound of the trump, saying: Fear God, and give glory to him who sitteth upon the throne, forever and ever; for the hour of his judgment is come.

D&C 88:104

*R*obert Louis Stevenson said, "To be what we are, and to become what we are capable of becoming, is the only end of life" (in *Familiar Studies of Men and Books*, London: Chatto and Windus, 1882).

The gospel calls to us to stretch ourselves, to embrace our talents, to concentrate on our strengths, to be productive, to be creative, to reach our full potential, which few of us ever do. We seem to get discouraged by such trivial things and fail to see the great things we are capable of doing.

O human race, born to fly upward, wherefore at a little wind dost thou so fall?

Dante Alighieri
The Divine Comedy, "Purgatorio," xii, 95

*M*aking soup is especially satisfying on a cold, wintry day. This is an easy favorite.

Clam Chowder

Combine the following and heat in a heavy saucepan:

ingredients

¹/₂ to 1 cup bacon, fried and crumbled

2 large potatoes, peeled, boiled, and diced

1 (10.75-oz.) can cream of celery soup

1 (6.5-oz.) can clams, undrained

1 (14.75-oz.) can corn (or use frozen), drained

1 heaping tablespoon butter

The key to enjoying cooking is embracing simplicity. Simplicity in food is honesty, warmth, pleasure, modesty, even fairness. Simplicity in cooking is ease and grace. . . . Simplicity . . . is not a compromise but a treasure.

Mark Bittman
The Minimalist Cooks at Home
(New York: Broadway Books, 1999).

*O*ne fall afternoon Brother Hinckley and I stepped off a plane in Athens, Greece. At the airport to meet us were a Latter-day Saint woman and her husband from Idaho who were on a two-year teaching assignment in Athens. (The Church was not officially recognized or organized in Greece at the time.) We explained to them that we would be there only about twenty hours and inquired if there was anything they needed or anything we could do for them.

The sister spoke up and said, "Couldn't we just hold a Latter-day Saint meeting: have a prayer, sing the songs of Zion, and have some talks?" So that night we met in their apartment. They invited three well-dressed Indian women and two young American men. We sat in a circle and began the meeting. We sang the opening song; an opening prayer was offered, and then we sang another hymn. It was then that I noticed the tears welling up in my new friend's eyes. She leaned over to me and said, "Oh, you'll just have to pardon me. You don't know how wonderful it is just to be sitting in a Latter-day Saint meeting. I miss it so much."

Since then, each time I sit in a Latter-day Saint meeting, whether it be a sacrament meeting, a Relief Society meeting, a leadership meeting, or a Sunday School class, I say a quiet prayer to my Heavenly Father, thanking Him for just being able to meet with my friends in the name of the Lord.

And the church did meet together oft to fast and to pray, and to speak one with another concerning the welfare of their souls.

Moroni 6:5

*L*ife is full of challenges. Many of them involve balance and temperance. Complete abstention may be much easier than moderation. It's easier for me to completely abstain from smoking than to try to balance my day—a little for this, a little for that, a little for him, a little for her.

Ralph Waldo Emerson expressed a majestic thought when he said: "It is easy in the world to live after the world's opinion; it is easy in solitude to live after our own; but the great man is he who in the midst of the crowd keeps with perfect sweetness the independence of solitude."

I know it is hard for you young mothers to believe that almost before you can turn around the children will be gone and you will be alone with your husband. You had better be sure you are developing the kind of love and friendship that will be delightful and enduring. Let the children learn from your attitude that he is important. Encourage him. Be kind. It is a rough world, and he, like everyone else, is fighting to survive. Be cheerful. Don't be a whiner.

Marriage is still very much a living institution, worth all the time and patience invested in it. Marriage is the stable structure that encircles and supports two clumsy individuals, learning to love and live with each other.

Ronna Romney and Beppie Harrison
Giving Time a Chance
(New York: Bantam Books, 1983), 287–88

*E*ither Joseph Smith had a vision or he didn't. If he did not, then we are all engaged in a tremendous hoax; but if he did, then it behooves each of us to give all the time, money, effort, and energy we can muster to promote the kingdom of God.

Therefore, O ye that embark in the service of God, see that ye serve him with all your heart, might, mind and strength, that ye may stand blameless before God at the last day.

D&C 4:2

It's a valuable exercise to close your eyes every once in a while and think, "What is the most wonderful moment I have lived through during the past year?"

It might be part of a grand event or a very simple moment, perhaps a brief interaction with another person. The grand or the simple, it doesn't matter. Just the remembering will lift your spirits, and warm feelings will fill your soul.

Try to remember,
and if you remember,
Then follow.

Tom Jones

*F*ind joy in your children. Don't overschedule them or yourself. You may not be able to take them on exotic vacations. It doesn't matter. When the day dawns bright and sunny, take an excursion to the canyon or the park. When it's cloudy and wet, read a book together or make something good to eat. Give them time to explore and learn about the feel of grass and the wiggliness of worms.

When the voices of children are heard on the green
And laughing is heard on the hill,
My heart is at rest within my breast
And everything else is still.

William Blake, "Nurse's Song," st. 1

I love music—all kinds. When I was in high school there used to be a ward dance every Thursday night. We walked to the church, and when we turned the corner on 8th East we could hear the orchestra and we would break into a run, so excited were we to hear the music. It was just about the only music we heard from Thursday to Thursday, outside of the two or three phonograph records we owned—one of Caruso and the other a violin recording by Kreisler. When our children were growing up our home was full of music: Broadway soundtracks, jazz, folk music, religious music, classical music. Music alone can do much to create a rich and positive atmosphere in a home. Even now I move from room to room in our apartment and I can hear music from every corner. What a wonderful world!

*W*e are God's children, and if we ever got that through our heads thoroughly and understood that completely, we would never do a small thing, we would never say a cross word. We would not use bad language. We would not criticize anybody. We would love everyone the way the Savior loves us. "As I have loved you, love one another."

That by him, and through him, and of him, the worlds are and were created, and the inhabitants thereof are begotten sons and daughters unto God

D&C 76:24

$\mathcal{I}$ decided that if I lived to be eighty-five I would stop counting calories and eat anything I wanted to eat. And I do!

I would make my mother's lemon pie, but I have quit cooking too!

Lemon Pie Filling

3 tablespoons flour
3 tablespoons cornstarch
1 cup sugar
Pinch of salt
1½ cups boiling water
2 egg yolks, beaten
Juice and grated rind of 1 lemon

recipe directions

Mix flour, cornstarch, sugar, and salt. Add water. Boil 10 minutes, stirring constantly. Stir in egg yolks, heat thoroughly. Add lemon juice and rind; Remove from heat, cool, and pour into baked crust. Top with meringue if desired.

$\mathcal{T}$hink about your particular assignment at this time in your life. It may be to get an education, it may be to rear children in righteousness, it may be to be a grandparent, it may be to care for and relieve the suffering of someone you love, it may be to do a job in the most excellent way possible, it may be to support someone who has a difficult assignment of their own. Our assignments are varied and they change from time to time. Don't take them lightly. Give them your full heart and energy. Do them with enthusiasm. Do whatever you have to do this week with your whole heart and soul. To do less than this will leave you with an empty feeling.

Nothing great was ever achieved without enthusiasm.

Ralph Waldo Emerson
Essays: First Series, "Circles" (1841)

*T*here is something about spirituality that is central to the life of a woman. Not the kind of spirituality that only takes you to church on Sunday. I am talking about the kind of spirituality that makes you behave like a child of God.

Be steadfast and immovable, always abounding in good works, that Christ, the Lord God Omnipotent, may seal you his that you may be brought to heaven, that ye may have everlasting salvation and eternal life, through the wisdom, and power, and justice, and mercy of him who created all things, in heaven and in earth, who is God above all.

Mosiah 5:15

A testimony is something we must get through the Holy Ghost. If one person could give it to another, all parents who possessed it would give it to their children. It cannot be bought with money. It can be had only when we have made ourselves worthy and have sought the Lord in humility and diligence. Then it will surely be ours.

Yea, behold, I will tell you in your mind
and in your heart, by the Holy Ghost,
which shall come upon you and which
shall dwell in your heart.

D&C 8:2

*F*ifty was my favorite age. It takes about that long to learn to quit competing—to be yourself and settle down to living. It is the age I would like to be through all eternity!

It is difficult to make a man miserable while he feels he is worthy of himself and claims kindred to the great God who made him.

Abraham Lincoln, 1862.

$\mathcal{A}$s a resurrected and glorified being, giving His last instructions to His disciples, the Savior spoke words of reassurance: "I will not leave you comfortless: I will come to you" (John 14:18). And then as we take that sentence and continue with His invitation from the scriptures, "Come, follow me," we understand more completely. What better way to follow Him than to comfort one another?

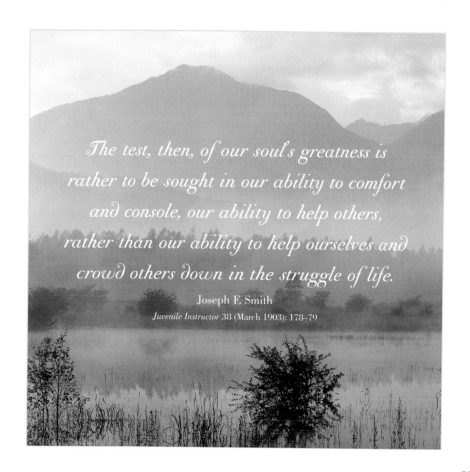

*The test, then, of our soul's greatness is
rather to be sought in our ability to comfort
and console, our ability to help others,
rather than our ability to help ourselves and
crowd others down in the struggle of life.*

Joseph F. Smith

Juvenile Instructor 38 (March 1903): 178–79

We all have a responsibility—a responsibility to make a difference, to be an influence, to lift someone. We are all in this together to work out our salvation, to reach our potential, and to be our brother's keeper—to help each other.

The least of us, the humblest, is in partnership with the Almighty in achieving the purpose of the eternal plan of salvation. That places us in a very responsible attitude toward the human race.

John A. Widtsoe

Utah Genealogical and Historical Magazine 25 (October 1934): 189

Feast upon the words of Christ.

2 Nephi 32:3

I love the word *feast*. We talk about *pondering* the scriptures, but I like the phrase "feast upon the words."

J have two choices. I can choose to be happy or I can choose to be sad. I choose to be happy. "For the power is in them, wherein they are agents unto themselves" (D&C 58:28).

The greatest gift that God in his bounty made in creation, and the most conformable to his goodness, and that which he prizes the most, was the freedom of the will, with which the creatures with intelligence, they all and they alone, were and are endowed.

Dante Alighieri
The Divine Comedy, "Paradiso," v, 19

*E*ach day brings its own challenges, but life would be a total waste without knowing what it is all about and where we can get help.

And lo, I am with thee,
even unto the end of thy days.

Moses 1:26

It was while I was still very young that I made up my mind I would stay true and faithful to the gospel so that the suffering of my pioneer ancestors would not have been in vain. I know that the day will come when I will see them. How can I face them if I have not built on the foundation they have laid?

When you are in your nineties you find that many of your dear friends have gone on. But even with these separations, my love for them remains intact and I look forward to renewing those close relationships. How grateful I am for the gospel and for the assurance that even friendships are eternal.

Each life that touches ours for good
Reflects thine own great mercy, Lord;
Thou sendest blessings from above
Thru words and deeds of those who love. . . .

When such a friend from us departs,
We hold forever in our hearts
A sweet and hallowed memory,
Bringing us nearer, Lord, to thee.

Karen Lynn Davidson
"Each Life That Touches Ours for Good," *Hymns*, no. 293

I like the smell of dinner baking in the oven. Maybe it's the closest I will ever come to experiencing the fulfillment of the scripture: "If ye are prepared ye shall not fear" (D&C 38:30).

Stuffed Green Peppers

1 ½ cups tomato juice
½ cup uncooked rice
2 tablespoons chopped onion
½ pound extra lean ground beef, uncooked
½ cup grated cheese (or to taste)
Salt and pepper to taste
4 green peppers

recipe directions

Place tomato juice, rice, and onion in a pan over low heat. Cover and simmer until juice is absorbed (about 20 minutes). Combine rice mixture with ground beef, cheese, salt, and pepper and fill green peppers (slice off tops and seed). Place in casserole or pan with lid and bake at 300° F. for one hour.

Be kind. Everyone you meet is fighting a hard battle.

No act of kindness, no matter how small, is ever wasted.

Aesop, *The Lion and the Mouse*

*I*t's nice to be smart, but it doesn't mean much unless you work hard. Working hard is even better than being smart!

There is no substitute for hard work. . . .
Genius is one per cent inspiration and
ninety-nine per cent perspiration.

Thomas Alva Edison

*E*ducation, formal education, is a wonderful thing. No matter the class you may choose to take, learn. Learn as if your life depended on it. Perhaps it will. When you open a new textbook, say to yourself, "I want to know what this book has to teach me." Learn the thrill of digging for fossils on the mountainside, or working over a test tube until dark, or getting on the trail of something in the library and searching it down feverishly for hours. Be a real student, an intellectually curious student.

How can we know if this gospel is a thing of God if we do not do the works of God? The only way we can know whether or not this is the true church is to try it out for ourselves. Until we give it a fair chance, we are hardly in a position to pass judgment. We will come to know that the gospel is true by trying it out.

If any man will do his will, he shall know of the doctrine, whether it be of God, or whether I speak of myself.

John 7:17

74

We each do the best we can. My best may not be as good as your best, but it's my best. The fact is that we know when we are doing our best and when we are not. If we are not doing our best, it leaves us with a gnawing hunger and frustration. But when we do our level best, we experience a peace.

*A*s you create a home, don't get distracted with a lot of things that have no meaning for either you or your family. Don't dwell on your failures, but think about your successes.

I know of no more encouraging
fact than the unquestionable ability of man to
elevate his life by a conscious endeavor.

Henry David Thoreau,
"Where I Lived and What I Lived For," *Walden*
(New York: Bantam Books, 1982), 172

$\mathcal{E}$ach of us can ask ourselves each morning, "What can I do to make life happier for someone today?"

What do we live for, if it is not to make life less difficult for each other?

George Elliot
Middlemarch
(New York: Penguin Books, 1994), 789

$\mathcal{B}$eing a mother at any age is a blessing, but as we age and our children become interesting and productive adults we really begin to savor the joys of the harvest, the fruit of our labors. How could we have known when they were young and the demands so constant that we would ever have the luxury of simply enjoying their loving companionship?

Then, . . . ye shall reap the rewards of your faith, and your diligence, and patience, and long-suffering, waiting for the tree to bring forth fruit unto you.

Alma 32:43

$\mathcal{T}$rue spirituality makes you loving and grateful, and forgiving, and patient, and gentle, and long-suffering. True spirituality breathes reverence into every act and deed. It compels you to get in touch with your Heavenly Father every single day of your life.

Be meek and lowly in heart . . . cry unto God for all thy support; yea, let all thy doings be unto the Lord, and whithersoever thou goest let it be in the Lord; yea, let all thy thoughts be directed unto the Lord; yea, let the affections of thy heart be placed upon the Lord forever.

Alma 37:34, 36

We have our work cut out for us. We have a very important role to play in the building up of God's kingdom. We do not have to walk the dusty plains and live in undesirable dwellings and fight off mobs and hostile Indians, but we have our own little battles to fight.

I have commanded you to organize yourselves . . .
For the purpose of building up my church and kingdom
on the earth, and to prepare my people for the time
when I shall dwell with them, which is nigh at hand.

D&C 104:58, 59

The thing about growing old is that when you wake up with a new pain, you can just about count on it becoming a permanent part of your life!

It's a common saying, but one that gives us heart: "When the going gets tough, the tough get going." When trials and tribulations come, we can just hang tight and keep doing our best and things will eventually get better.

And not only so, but we glory in tribulations also: knowing that tribulation worketh patience.

Romans 5:3

I got this recipe from a Japanese member of the Okinawa Relief Society many years ago. It's a bit of work, but it's good!

Sweet and Sour Pork

recipe directions

Cut one pound of pork into ³/₄-inch cubes and mix with 1 tablespoon cornstarch, 2 tablespoons flour, 1 egg white, and a little salt. Fry pork in deep, hot fat until brown; set aside

For sauce, combine ¹/₂ cup sugar and 1¹/₂ tablespoons cornstarch. Stir into ¹/₃ cup vinegar and ²/₃ cup water. Whisk to remove any lumps. Cook over medium heat until thickened, stirring constantly. Set aside.

Heat another pan. Using 3 tablespoons oil, sauté ¹/₂ cup sliced onion, ¹/₂ cup sliced carrots (sliced lengthwise with a vegetable peeler), 1 sliced green pepper, and a cucumber cut in long strips. Don't overcook vegetables. They should remain rather crisp.

Combine ¹/₂ cup pineapple chunks, the sautéed vegetables, the fried pork, and the sweet and sour sauce. Stir in 4 tablespoons tomato catsup. Mix thoroughly and serve hot with rice.

Food is so pleasurable and powerful that it plays an essential role in creating a home that works. For your home to feel solid, meaningful, dignified, and warm, you must have the means and skills to produce good, nutritious food, to dream up pleasant menus, and to set the table and serve the food in an attractive manner that is familiar and comfortable to guests.

Cheryl Mendelson

Home Comforts: The Art and Science of Keeping House
(New York: Scribner, 1999), 33

*T*here is a solemness and sacredness about a sacrament meeting. It is different from any other meeting held in the Church.

And as they were eating, Jesus took bread, and blessed it, and brake it, and gave it to the disciples, and said, Take, eat; this is my body.

And he took the cup, and gave thanks, and gave it to them, saying, Drink ye all of it; For this is my blood of the new testament, which is shed for many for the remission of sins.

Matthew 26:26–28

Scriptures are needed more and more as the years rush by. They become more and more meaningful because we have more and more experiences that help us to relate to them.

I did liken all scriptures
unto us, that it might be for
our profit and learning.

1 Nephi 19:23

*H*ow simple it is, really, to extend a kindness when we see the need. Jesus set the example on many occasions. He led the blind man out of the town. Just a small kindness, but a powerful example. God helps us to recognize the opportunities we have every day to touch lives in small and simple ways.

*And he took the blind man
by the hand, and led him
out of the town.*

Mark 8:23

Keep the faith. It pays such great dividends!

They that wait upon the Lord shall renew their strength;
they shall mount up with wings as eagles; they shall run,
and not be weary; and they shall walk, and not faint.

Isaiah 40:31

There are some years in our lives that we would not want to live again. But even these years will pass away, and the lessons learned will be a future blessing.

*Be patient in afflictions, for
thou shalt have many but endure
them, for, lo, I am with thee,
even unto the end of thy days.*

D&C 24:8

I love the scripture in Mosiah:

"And see that all these things are done in wisdom and order; for it is not requisite that a man should run faster than he has strength. And again, it is expedient that he should be diligent, that thereby he might win the prize; therefore, all things must be done in order."

Mosiah 4:27

Choose carefully each day that which you will do and that which you will not do, and the Lord will bless you to accomplish the important things that have eternal consequences. At my age, I've edited the scripture just a little: "For it is not requisite that a woman should hobble faster than she has strength!"

*T*he trouble with the world and the trouble with you and me is that we don't love each other enough. And if we do, we don't bother to show it, or we don't bother to say it. If the world is to know love, it has to be in your heart and in mine. And the Lord can fill our hearts with love if we will just go to Him.

Pray unto the Father with all the energy of heart, that ye may be filled with this love, which he hath bestowed upon all who are true followers of his Son, Jesus Christ.

Moroni 7:48

A prophet has been described as a great torchlight striding through the earth lighting the lamps of truth. Your candle has been lit; mine has been lit; it is up to us to keep the flame burning and thereby light many more.

> *We thank thee, O God, for a prophet*
> *To guide us in these latter days.*
> *We thank thee for sending the gospel*
> *To lighten our minds with its rays.*

William Fowler
"We Thank Thee, O God, for a Prophet" *Hymns*, no. 19

*S*weet reminders of good times are dishes on the table that were first tasted in someone else's home. Here's one from a mission home in Tokyo, Japan.

Teriyaki Steak

recipe directions

Ask the butcher to cut a sirloin tip roast into thin slices. Marinate meat for several hours in the following mixture:

1 clove chopped garlic

2 tablespoons sugar

4 tablespoons soy sauce

1/4 teaspoon fresh grated gingerroot

Fry quickly in a generous amount of hot vegetable oil. Good served with Cucumber Relish.

Cucumber Relish

8 small cucumbers, cut lengthwise in wedges, seeds discarded
1 carrot, sliced thinly with vegetable peeler

recipe directions

Soak in salted water for 10 minutes. Drain. Cover with:

$1/4$ cup vinegar

$3/4$ cup water

Sugar to taste

$\mathcal{M}$y mother always said that she didn't mind getting old herself, but she couldn't stand to see her children get old!

And it came to pass that I, Jacob, began to be old; . . .
the time passed away with us, and also our lives passed
away like as it were unto us a dream.

Jacob 7:26

The road has not been paved all the way for any of us. We all have a small place in our hearts where we store our sorrows and disappointments. But are there not days when you are simply overwhelmed with the blessings of the Lord? It was ever thus.

I, Nephi, having been born of
goodly parents . . . having seen many
afflictions in the course of my days,
nevertheless, having been highly
favored of the Lord in all my days

1 Nephi 1:1

*T*he light of Christ brings peace to the troubled mind, rest to the weary, solace to those in sorrow, and joy to those who walk uprightly.

But the fruit of the Spirit is love, joy, peace, longsuffering, gentleness, goodness, faith.
Galatians 5:22

117

My mother taught me some basic philosophies of rearing children. One is that you have to trust them. I tried hard never to say "no" if I could possibly say "yes." I think that worked well because it gave my children the feeling that I trusted them and they were responsible to do the best they could.

I love the sights and sounds and smells of a bustling city in a foreign country. I love the peaceful green hills of the countryside. I love the color of autumn leaves against a deep blue sky, the sound of a bird, the scent of pines. I love the sight of temple spires reaching into the heavens. Every day brings something beautiful if we are just willing to look up and see it.

God's World

O world, I cannot hold thee close enough!
Thy winds, thy wide grey skies!
Thy mists, that roll and rise!
Thy woods, this autumn day, that ache and sag
And all but cry with colour! That gaunt crag
To crush! To lift the lean of that black bluff!
World, World, I cannot get thee close enough!

Long have I known a glory in it all,
But never knew I this:
Here such a passion is
As stretcheth me apart,—Lord, I do fear
Thou'st made the world too beautiful this year.
My soul is all but out of me—let fall
No burning leaf; prithee, let no bird call.

Edna St. Vincent Millay

Collected Poems of Edna St. Vincent Millay,
Norma Millay, ed. (New York: Harper & Bros, 1956), 32

I can only thank my Father in Heaven for wonderful and unusual opportunities. I know that where much is given, much is expected. And that is a frightening thought.

For of him unto whom much is given much is required; and he who sins against the greater light shall receive the greater condemnation.

D&C 82:3

*O*ur testimonies have to be renewed every day. Sometimes they are renewed simply because of a little experience, or maybe reading a verse of scripture that touches a tender spot, or turning a corner and coming upon a field of wildflowers, or seeing a newborn babe—perfect in every way. But renewal mostly comes from living the gospel and serving in the Church. It isn't so hard to renew your testimony daily if you are active in the Church. As President David O. McKay said, "It comes as a natural sequence to the performance of duty."

And behold, as the tree beginneth to grow, ye will say: Let us nourish it with great care, that it may get root, that it may grow up, and bring forth fruit unto us.

Alma 32:37

*E*lder Neal A. Maxwell once said, "We are here in mortality, and the only way to go is through; there isn't any around!" (*Ensign,* May 1998, 9). I would add, the only way to get through life is to laugh your way through it. You either have to laugh or cry. I prefer to laugh. Crying gives me a headache.

Laugh, and the world laughs with you;
Weep, and you weep alone;
For the sad old earth must borrow its mirth,
But has trouble enough of its own.

Ella Wheeler Wilcox, "Solitude," st. 1

*F*rom a kitchen in Parowan, Utah. Many of my granddaughters still make these for their young families.

Refrigerator Bran Muffins

2 cups boiling water

6 cups Kellogg's® All-Bran cereal

1 cup shortening

1½ cups sugar

4 eggs

1 quart buttermilk

5 cups flour

5 teaspoons baking soda—sift this into flour to remove any lumps

1 teaspoon salt

recipe ∂*irections*

Pour boiling water over bran in large bowl. Add shortening. Stir until short-ening is melted and let cool. Add other ingredients. Stir to mix well. Use immediately, or cover and put in refrigerator and bake as desired. Batter will keep in refrigerator up to two weeks.

Drop by spoonfuls into well-greased muffin pans. Bake at 400° F. for about 10 minutes. Test with a toothpick for doneness.

> *The [kitchen] table is where we mark milestones,*
> *divulge dreams, bury hatchets, make deals, give*
> *thanks, plan vacations, and tell jokes. It's also where*
> *children learn the lessons that families teach: manners,*
> *cooperation, communication, self-control, values.*

Doris Christopher
Come to the Table: A Celebration of Family Life
(New York: Warner Books, 1999), 2–3

Try, as husbands and wives, not to be too demanding of one another. There must be a little give and take, a great deal of flexibility, and fierce loyalty to make a happy home.

Therefore shall a man leave his father
and his mother, and shall cleave unto his wife:
and they shall be one flesh.

Genesis 2:24

We are all in this together. We need each other, Oh, how we need each other. Those of us who are old need you who are young. And, hopefully, you who are young need some of us who are old. It is a sociological fact that women need women. We need deep and satisfying and loyal friendships with each other. These friendships are a necessary source of sustenance. We need to renew our faith every day. We need to lock arms and help build the kingdom so that it will roll forth and fill the whole earth.

That I may be comforted
together with you by the mutual
faith both of you and me.

Romans 1:12

*T*ravel is wonderful, but if you do very much of it, the places all become a blur. But the people—when you get wherever you're going and begin to meet the people, you come alive again. People are wonderful. Each one has a story, each something to give, each knows something interesting, something that can make your life richer.

Man is in reality a child of God.
Nothing in the universe is more
important than the individual.
His spirit was begotten of God;
consequently all men are brothers
in the literal sense.

Gordon B. Hinckley
Teachings of Gordon B. Hinckley
(Salt Lake City: Deseret Book, 1997), 159

One of the ablest women in this country, now the wife of a university president, was brought up in poverty. She recalls an occasion when, as a girl, she complained of her hardships to her mother. "See here," said the mother. "I have given you life. That is probably all I will ever be able to give you. Now you stop complaining and do something with it."

Each of us has some things we could complain about, but what good would it do? Complaining seldom changes anything.

For ye shall go out with joy, and be led forth with peace: the mountains and the hills shall break forth before you into singing, and all the trees of the field shall clap their hands.

Isaiah 55:12

A merry heart doeth good like a medicine: but a broken spirit drieth the bones.

Proverbs 17:22

*G*od is what He is because He knows everything. And the beautiful thing— perhaps the thing I love most about the gospel—is that everything we learn we can use and take with us and use it again. No bit of knowledge goes wasted. Everything you are learning now is preparing you for something else. Did you know that? What a concept!

Seek ye diligently and teach one another words of wisdom; yea, seek ye out of the best books words of wisdom; seek learning, even by study and also by faith.
D&C 88:118

*C*hildren rise higher when they are treated with respect. Use courteous and respectful language when you talk with your children and others. Bruno Bettelheim, a world-famous psychologist, said, "You can't teach children to be good. The best you can do for your child is to live a good life yourself. What a parent knows and believes, the child will lean on." You don't teach a child not to yell by yelling. We cannot expect to be respected if we treat others in demeaning ways.

And let every man esteem his brother as himself, and practise virtue and holiness before me.

D&C 38:24

During World War II, we were encouraged to plant gardens, not only by the Church but by the government. My husband dug three thousand holes in the property to the south of our home and planted three thousand tomato plants. He hoed them and weeded them and irrigated them at 4:30 every Monday morning. When the tomatoes were ripe, I spent my days picking them. Baskets full, boxes full. We put up a sign: "Tomatoes for Sale." Toward the end of the crop, we couldn't give them away. My back ached.

I could have said, "Is this what I was born to do?"

But the tomatoes went on people's food shelves, and the money we were paid for them paid the taxes that year—the taxes on our house, the house that gave us shelter and was a home for our children. The whole project gave my husband and me a sense of "togetherness."

*O*ftentimes the thing that makes the difference between a good student and a poor one, a good learner or a bored human being, is just a little curiosity. If you have it, cultivate it, feed it. Never let it go. If you do not have it—get it. Wonder, watch, ask questions, be alive. It's just that simple.

Ammaron said to the ten-year-old-boy Mormon: "I perceive that thou art a sober child, and art quick to observe" (Mormon 1:2). Could that quickness to observe be what we are talking about—an innate curiosity about people, events, and the world?

In the book of Alma is a story that has fascinated me since I first read it. It is about a very colorful character named Moroni—not to be confused with the last survivor of the Nephites, who was also named Moroni. This man was a brilliant military commander, and he rose to be supreme commander of all the Nephite forces at the age of twenty-five. For the next fourteen years he was off to the wars continuously except for two very short periods of peace during which he worked feverishly at reinforcing the Nephite defenses. When peace finally came, he was thirty-nine years old, and the story goes that at the age of forty-three he died. Sometime before this he had given the chief command of the armies of the Nephites to his son Moronihah. Now, if he had a son, he had a wife. I've often wondered where she was and how she fared during those fourteen years of almost continuous warfare, and how she felt to have him die so soon after coming home. I am sure there are many, many stories of patience and sacrifice that have never been told. We each do our part, and we each have our story.

We women have a lot to learn about simplifying our lives. We have to decide what is important and then move along at a pace that is comfortable for us. We have to develop the maturity to stop trying to prove something. We have to learn to be content with what we are.

For all have not every gift given unto them; for there are many gifts, and to every man [and woman] is given a gift by the Spirit of God. To some is given one, and to some is given another, that all may be profited thereby.

D&C 46:11–12

The family is eternal. Love must be nurtured. It must be spoken. We must put away our pride, our haughtiness, our shyness, our misunderstandings, and with humility say, "I love you. Is there something I can do to help you?" You can never be completely happy under any other circumstances.

*I know that we came to this life with a purpose and
that the greatest joy we will receive will be those
acts of love and service that we do for others. . . .
There is none too great to need the help of others.
There is none so great that he can "do it alone."*

Robert D. Hales

Ensign, November 1975, 93.

*I*t is for us to go about our work, making certain that underlying everything we do in the course of a day is a settled faith in God, in His existence, personality, and attributes. This faith will give us the power to work righteousness.

If I am in the line of my duty, I am doing the will of God, whether I am preaching; praying; laboring with my hands for an honorable support; whether I am in the field, mechanic's shop, or following mercantile business, or wherever duty calls, I am serving God as much in one place as another; and so it is with all, each in his place, turn and time.

Brigham Young
Journal of Discourses, 13:261

*G*od bless us to do those small and simple
things that need to be done by our hands
and to do them all with a cheerful heart.

The reward of a thing well done, is to have done it.

Ralph Waldo Emerson

Essays: Second Series, "Nominalist and Realist," 1844